Introduction

Welcome to *Felt From The Heart*, featuring more than twenty-four wonderful handmade stuffed animals, creatures, and veggies, plus cute habitats for all your creations to hang out in. Sewing is my first love in the crafting world, and I want to get you, the beginner sewer, started. Every project in this book is sewn by hand using only embroidery floss and eight different stitches (see the Embroidery Stitch Guide on page 2). Additionally, each of these projects has a heart incorporated into the design, because each project is made from the heart. You will find this book provides you with two secret weapons to help keep these projects simple and quick: the stretch glove and iron-on adhesive. See my tips on this page for more information, or visit my website *www.whencreativityknocks.com* for more craft ideas and advice.

—Ana

ISBN 978-1-57421-365-2

© 2013 by Ana Araujo and Design Originals, *www.d-originals.com*, an imprint of Fox Chapel Publishing, 800-457-9112, 1970 Broad Street, East Petersburg, PA 17520.

Printed in China
First printing

Recommended Supplies

I recommend the following supplies to complete these projects. Substitute your choice of brands, tools, and materials as desired.

- ◆ Clover Needlecraft, Inc. products
  - —Gold Eye Embroidery Needles
  - —Patchwork Pins
  - —Patchwork Scissors
  - —Pom-Pom Maker, small
- ◆ National Nonwovens wool blend felt
- ◆ DMC embroidery floss
- ◆ Heat 'n Bond Lite iron-on adhesive
- ◆ Beacon Fabric-Tac fabric glue
- ◆ Favorite Findings buttons
- ◆ Rit dye
- ◆ The Bandanna Company bandannas

Acknowledgements

A special thank you to the following people who helped make *Felt From The Heart* so heartwarming:

The adorable toddler models—my grandson Charlie Niczewicz, The Aileen Boy, and Avery Koch, the most yummy Cupcake Princess ever!

To Sarah Bauerle for her patience while taking the photos of the toddlers and her good eye behind the camera.

The use of the QR code in this book would not have been possible without the help of Scott Pfeiffer.

To my personal editor, Susan Hare, and to National Nonwovens, who provided all the felt for this book. And last, but not least, to my crafting sidekick Cindi Bisson.

Embroidery Stitch Guide

The running, back, and stem stitches illustrated below are used for mouths and detail work. The whip and blanket stitches are used to bind front and back pieces together along the edges. The satin stitch is used for noses and the French knot for tiny eyes. The eyelash stitch is a new stitch that was created for this book, because embroidered eyelashes don't always look even.

If you are a beginner, consider making a stitch guide like the one pictured at right to practice your stitches. Attach each square and heart to a larger piece of felt using the stitches illustrated on this page.

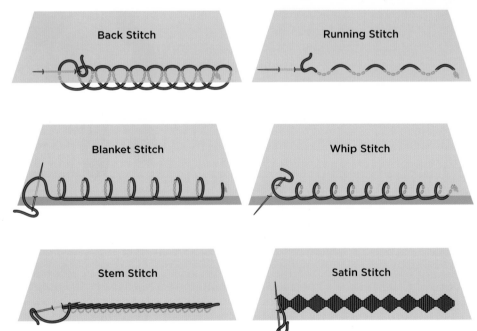

Back Stitch

Running Stitch

Blanket Stitch

Whip Stitch

Stem Stitch

Satin Stitch

French Knot

The eyelash stitch will allow you to add adorable face details to your felt creations. Follow the three easy steps shown for a great eyelash every time!

Ana's Tips

The felt

The key ingredient in all the projects is felt. I prefer wool, wool-rayon blended, or bamboo-rayon blended felt, but acrylic felt works fine as well. A special thank you to National Nonwovens for providing the felt for this book.

Embroidery floss

Embroidery floss consists of six strands of thread loosely twisted together. For these projects, cut a strand of embroidery floss to the length with which you want to sew. Then, carefully pull two strands of the thread away from the other four. All the projects in this book are stitched using two strands of thread. Be sure to purchase high-quality embroidery floss—it makes a difference during sewing and doesn't tangle as much as lower-quality floss.

Iron-on adhesive

Don't freak out when you see all the pieces for these projects! It looks like a lot of sewing, but using iron-on adhesive will help make every project super easy! Whenever you see the words "Heat set," use the following process to make an iron-on felt appliqué. Note: These instructions refer to Heat 'n Bond Lite iron-on adhesive. Be sure to refer to the manufacturer's instructions if using another product.

1. Cut a piece of felt and a piece of iron-on adhesive a little larger than the pattern piece.
2. Iron the adhesive to the felt piece following the manufacturer's directions, leaving the paper backing in place.
3. Cut out the pattern piece and trace it in reverse on the paper side of the iron-on adhesive with a pencil.
4. Following the pattern tracing, cut out the felt piece.
5. Peel off the paper backing and position the felt piece on the main felt body of the project.
6. Place a damp paper towel over the cutout and the main body. Press firmly for about 10–20 seconds. That's it! Super easy and quick!

The right scissors

I love scissors, and I have so many different kinds, but the ones I recommend for these projects are Clover Needlecraft Incorporated's Patchwork Scissors. They really cut all the little pieces well and produce a great, clean cut.

Secret Weapon: The Stretch Glove

The stretch glove is this book's secret weapon for making the arms, legs, and tails for all the felt critters. Cut the glove as shown.

The thumb and middle finger will form the legs, and the ring and pointer finger will form the arms. For creatures that need a tail, use the pinkie finger.

Although stretch gloves come in a variety of colors, you may not find the exact color you want every time. When this happens, you can dye a white or cream glove using a liquid dye, following the manufacturer's directions. Most dyes require the use of hot water. This will shrink your glove, but don't worry! The glove will stretch back to its normal size on your hand or when the fingers are stuffed.

Scan this code with your smart phone to see a video about using stretch gloves to make arms and legs for your felt creations.

Cupcake Princess

Every little girl wants to be a princess, but our little girl wants to be a cupcake princess! With her cupcake doll, scepter, and crown she will be ready to conquer any royal play kitchen in the kingdom!

Cupcake Princess Doll

This sweet-inspired doll will be adored by the sweet little ones in your life.

Patterns on page 10.

MATERIALS AND SUPPLIES:

- Felt in pink, purple, and red
- Purple stretch glove
- Embroidery thread in coordinating colors
- Embroidery needle
- Iron-on adhesive
- Two ½" (15mm) blue glitter buttons
- Bugle beads in assorted colors
- White rickrack
- 1 each, purple and pink glitter pom-poms
- Scissors
- Permanent marker
- Pins
- Polyester fiberfill stuffing

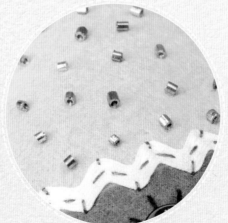

Cupcake Princess Doll (continued)

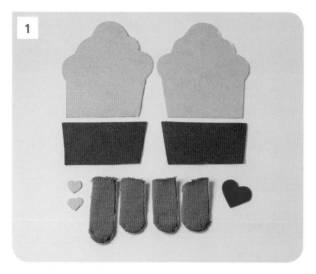

INSTRUCTIONS:

1 Prepare the pieces. Enlarge the pattern by the required amount and cut out all the pattern pieces. From the felt, cut two pink Doll bases, two purple Doll Wrappers, two pink Cheeks, and one red Heart. Mark the face details on the felt. From the purple glove, cut two arms and two legs.

2 Add the details. Heat set the cheeks, wrappers, and heart. Embroider the mouth, cheeks, eyelashes, button eyes, and white rickrack. Stitch or use fabric glue on the glitter pom-pom nose. Stitch the bugle beads onto the frosting area. Stuff the arms and legs.

3 Pin. Pin the front and back together, and pin the arms and legs in place.

4 Stitch, stuff, and finish. Whip stitch the doll together, leaving a small opening for stuffing. When stitching through the arms and legs, use a running stitch. Add a small amount of stuffing, and stitch the opening closed. Stitch the pink pom-pom on top.

Tank Top Bonus

To make this adorable Cupcake Princess tank top, follow the Cupcake Princess Doll directions, but only cut one body and one wrapper. Cut glove arms and legs, but don't stuff them. Whip stitch the cupcake to the front of a tank top. Stitch a button on the top of the cupcake and rickrack around tank top's neckline.

Cupcake Princess Scepter

This royal scepter is all that's needed
to rule the land of sweets and treats.

Patterns on page 10.

MATERIALS AND SUPPLIES:

- Felt in pink and purple
- Embroidery thread in coordinating colors
- Embroidery needle
- Iron-on adhesive
- Two ¼" (5mm) blue buttons
- White rickrack
- 1 each, purple and pink glitter pom-poms
- Bugle beads in assorted colors
- Several lengths of ribbon in pink and purple
- 1 wooden spoon
- Scissors
- Permanent marker
- Pins
- Polyester fiberfill stuffing

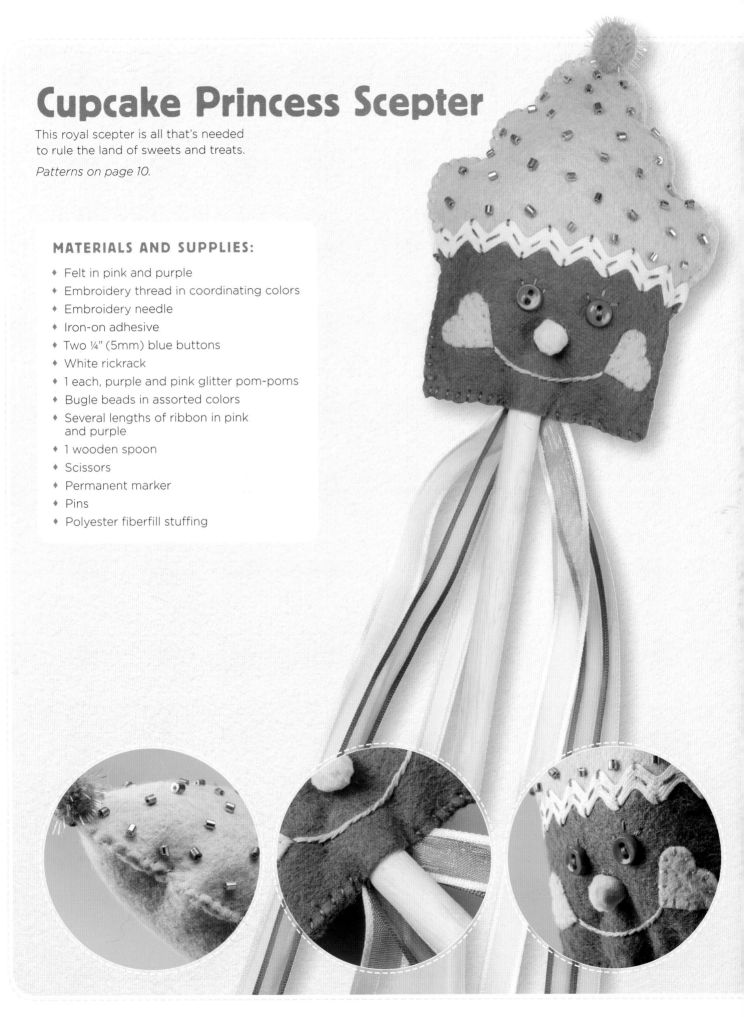

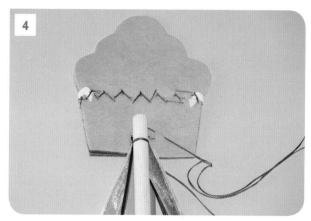

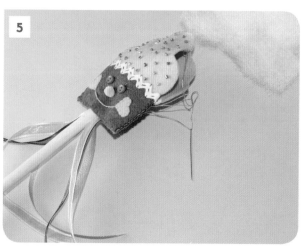

INSTRUCTIONS:

1 Prepare the pieces. Enlarge the pattern by the required amount and cut out all the pattern pieces. From the felt, cut two pink Scepter Bases, two purple Scepter Wrappers, and two Cheeks.

2 Heat set the necessary items. Heat set the checks and wrappers. Mark the face details on the felt.

3 Add the details. Embroider the mouth, cheeks, eyelashes, button eyes, and white rickrack. Stitch or glue on the glitter pom-pom nose. Stitch the bugle beads onto the frosting area.

4 Attach the ribbons and spoon. Stitch ribbons to the back side of the cupcake face, positioning them in the center of the cupcake. Then, place the handle of the wooden spoon over the ribbons, and stitch around the handle, catching the felt with each stitch.

5 Stitch, stuff, and finish. Pin the front and back pieces together. Stitch around the edges using a whip stitch, leaving a small opening for stuffing. Stuff the cupcake and stitch the opening closed. Stitch the purple pom-pom to the top.

Cupcake Princess Crown

Coronate your child or grandchild with this cupcake crown to make her feel like a true princess!

Patterns on page 10.

MATERIALS AND SUPPLIES:

- Felt in pink and purple
- Embroidery thread in coordinating colors
- Embroidery needle
- Iron-on adhesive
- 1 small pink pom-pom
- 4 small pink glitter pom-poms
- 1 large pink glitter pom-pom
- Bugle beads in assorted colors
- Several lengths of ribbon in pink and purple
- Eyelets
- Two ¼" (5mm) blue buttons
- Six ½" (15mm) purple glitter buttons
- Six ⅝" (15mm) pink glitter buttons
- Scissors
- Permanent marker

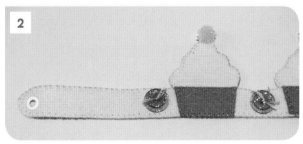

INSTRUCTIONS:

1 Prepare the pieces. Enlarge the pattern by the required amount and cut out all the pattern pieces. From the felt, cut one purple Crown Wrapper, four purple Mini-Wrappers, and two Cheeks. Using iron-on adhesive, attach a piece of purple felt to a piece of pink felt, creating a double-sided piece. Using the pattern, trace and cut the crown from the double-sided piece of felt.

2 Add the details and finish. Heat set the wrappers to the pink side of the crown, placing the large wrapper in the center. Blanket stitch around the edge of each cupcake's frosting area, and whip stitch around the edge of the crown. Stack the pink and purple buttons together and stitch them onto the crown in pairs between the cupcakes. On the center cupcake, embroider the mouth and cheeks, zigzag stitch along the top, sew on the button eyes and pom-pom nose, stitch the bugle beads onto the frosting area, and stitch the large pom-pom on top. Stitch the small glitter pom-poms to the top of each small cupcake. Add eyelets to each end of the crown and thread ribbon ties through them to hold the crown in place.

Cupcake Princess Patterns

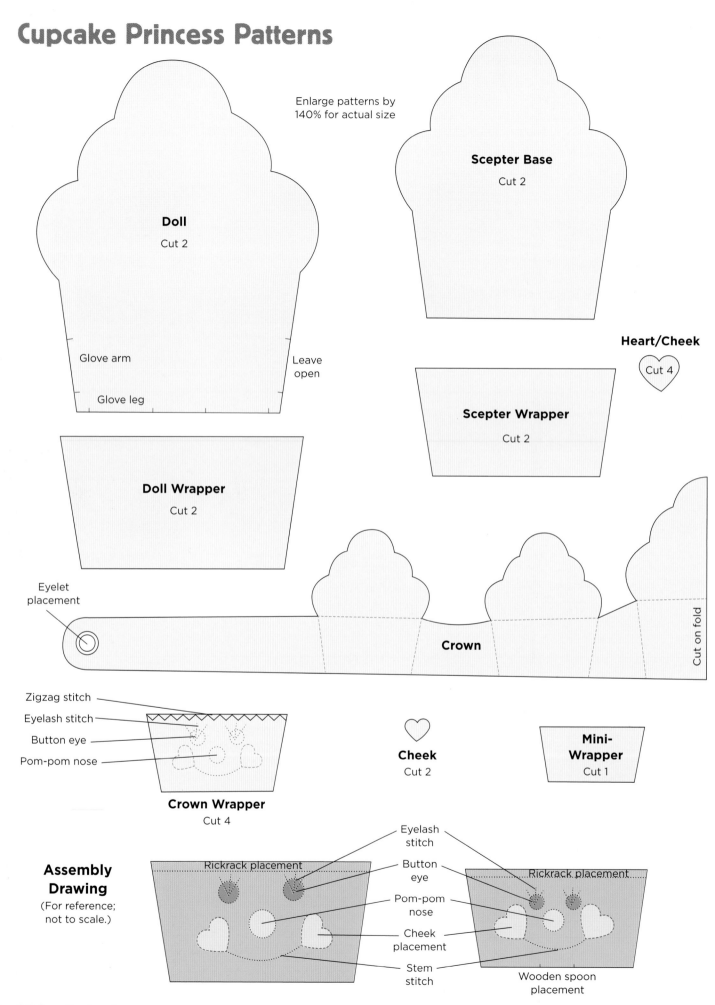

Enlarge patterns by 140% for actual size

Doll
Cut 2

Glove arm
Glove leg
Leave open

Scepter Base
Cut 2

Heart/Cheek
Cut 4

Scepter Wrapper
Cut 2

Doll Wrapper
Cut 2

Eyelet placement

Cut on fold

Crown

Zigzag stitch
Eyelash stitch
Button eye
Pom-pom nose

Crown Wrapper
Cut 4

Cheek
Cut 2

Mini-Wrapper
Cut 1

Assembly Drawing
(For reference; not to scale.)

Rickrack placement
Rickrack placement

Eyelash stitch
Button eye
Pom-pom nose
Cheek placement
Stem stitch

Wooden spoon placement

Little Boy's Alien Invasion

What little boy does not dream of going to space? With his alien doll, flying saucer, and alien headband, he is ready to blast off and fly to the moon!

Alien Boy Doll

This cute alien critter is perfect for the future space explorer in your life.

Patterns on page 18.

MATERIALS AND SUPPLIES:

- ♦ Felt in green, white, red, and gray
- ♦ Embroidery thread in coordinating colors
- ♦ Embroidery needle
- ♦ Iron-on adhesive
- ♦ Green stretch glove
- ♦ 2 pipe cleaners
- ♦ One $1\frac{9}{32}$" (15mm) green glitter button
- ♦ One $1\frac{5}{16}$" (25mm) black button
- ♦ 2 large green pom-poms
- ♦ Fabric glue
- ♦ Wire cutters
- ♦ Scissors
- ♦ Permanent marker
- ♦ Pins
- ♦ Polyester fiberfill stuffing

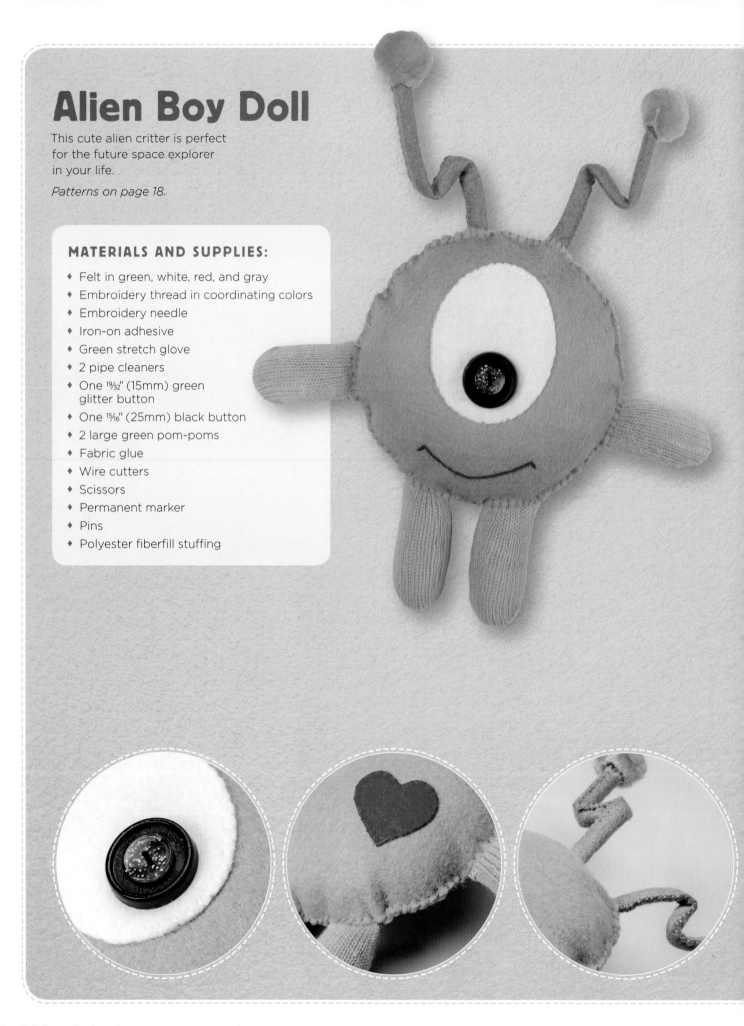

Alien Boy Doll (continued)

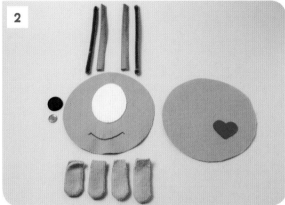

INSTRUCTIONS:

1 Prepare the pieces. Enlarge the pattern by the required amount and cut out all the pattern pieces. From the felt, cut two green Dolls, one white Eye, one red Heart, and two gray Antennae.

2 Add the details. Heat set the eye and heart. Stem stitch the mouth, and whip stitch around the edges of the eye and heart. Cut arms and legs from the green glove.

3 Create the antennae. Fold each antenna in half lengthwise and whip stitch along the long edge, leaving ends open. Cut two pipe cleaners to 5" (13cm) long. Fold back ¼" (5mm) of each end of the pipe cleaners. Slip one pipe cleaner into each antenna casing.

4 Add the eyeball and prepare for stitching. Stack a ¹⁹⁄₃₂" (15mm) green glitter button on top of a ¹⁵⁄₁₆" (25mm) black button. Stitch the buttons onto the eye to make an eyeball. Stuff the arms and legs. Pin the front and back pieces together, pinning the arms, legs, and antennae in place.

5 Stitch, stuff, and finish. Whip stitch the doll together, leaving a small opening for stuffing. When stitching through the arms and legs, use a running stitch. Add stuffing and stitch the opening closed. Using fabric glue, attach the large green pom-poms to the ends of the antennae. Bend the antennae into a zigzag shape.

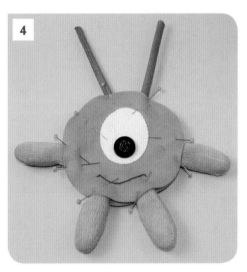

Alien Boy Flying Saucer

Count down to lift off, and send your alien doll into orbit with this stuffed spacecraft.

Patterns on page 19.

MATERIALS AND SUPPLIES:

♦ Felt in gray and yellow
♦ Embroidery thread in coordinating colors
♦ Embroidery needle
♦ Yellow hairband
♦ Ribbons in red and yellow
♦ Iron-on adhesive
♦ Silver rickrack
♦ 6 silver glitter star buttons
♦ Two ⅝" (15mm) yellow glitter buttons
♦ Four ⅝" (15mm) green glitter buttons
♦ One ¹⁹⁄₃₂" (15mm) yellow button
♦ One ¾" (20mm) red glitter button
♦ Fabric glue
♦ Scissors
♦ Permanent marker
♦ Pins
♦ Polyester fiberfill stuffing

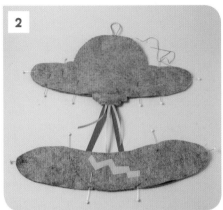

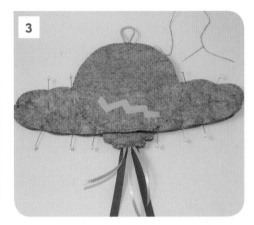

INSTRUCTIONS:

1 Prepare the pieces. Enlarge the pattern by the required amount and cut out all the pattern pieces. From the felt, cut two gray Flying Saucers, two gray Flying Saucer Dishes, and one yellow Lightning Bolt.

2 Create the separate parts. For the body of the flying saucer, pin the flying saucer front and back pieces together. Pin a yellow hairband in the center of the top of the flying saucer. Whip stitch around the top of the flying saucer, leaving an opening for stuffing. Pin red and yellow ribbon in between the front and back pieces at the engine of the flying saucer. Whip stitch around the engine's edges, stitching through the ribbons to hold them in place. Lightly stuff the engine and saucer bottom, and back stitch between the top of the engine and the bottom of the saucer. For the dish of the flying saucer, heat set the lightening bolt to the center of the dish. Pin the saucer dish front and back pieces together. Whip stitch along the top and bottom of the dish as marked on the pattern. Use a running back stitch as marked on the pattern to create the seat for the alien driver.

3 Stitch the parts together. Pin the saucer dish to the flying saucer body. Whip stitch through all four layers of felt on the dish/saucer sides, leaving small openings for stuffing as indicated on the pattern.

4 Stuff and stitch. Lightly stuff the saucer top and dish sides. Pin the openings and whip stitch them closed.

5 Add embellishments. Using fabric glue, attach sliver rickrack along the dish's edge. Stack silver glitter star buttons on top of ⅝" (15mm) yellow and green glitter buttons and stitch them in place. Stack a ¹⁹⁄₃₂" (15mm) yellow button on top of a ¾" (20mm) red glitter button and stitch them at the top of the saucer for a light.

Alien Boy Headband

When he dons this headband, your little one
will feel like he is from another planet.

Patterns on page 18.

MATERIALS AND SUPPLIES:

- Felt in green, gray, white, and yellow
- Embroidery thread in coordinating colors
- Embroidery needle
- Iron-on adhesive
- Silver rickrack
- 2 pipe cleaners
- 2 green pom-poms
- ¾" (20mm)-wide elastic band
- One $^{19}/_{32}$" (15mm) green glitter button
- One $^{15}/_{16}$" (25mm) black button
- Fabric glue
- Wire cutters
- Scissors
- Permanent marker

T-shirt Bonus

To make this Alien Boy t-shirt, follow the
Alien Boy Doll directions, but only cut
one body piece and two antennae. Cut
glove arms and legs, but don't stuff them.
Whip stitch the alien to the front of a
t-shirt, folding the felt for the antennae
into a zigzag. Stitch buttons at the top
of each antennae.

Alien Boy Headband (continued)

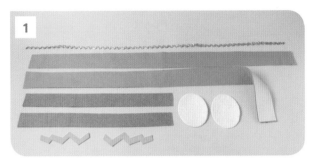

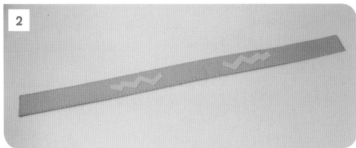

INSTRUCTIONS:

1 Prepare the pieces. Enlarge the pattern by the required amount and cut out all the pattern pieces. From the felt, cut two green Headbands, two gray Antennae (cut from one piece of felt, then fold it in half lengthwise and cut it to create two pieces), two white Eyes, and two yellow Lightning Bolts. Attach iron-on adhesive to one headband piece, one eyeball, and the lightning bolts. Cut a 20½″ (52cm)-long piece of sliver rickrack.

2 Create the headband. Heat set the headband pieces together. Heat set the lightening bolts to the headband as shown on the pattern. Whip stitch around the edges of the headband and lightening bolts.

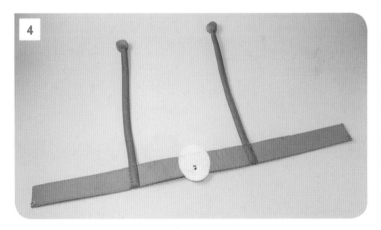

3 Create the antennae. Fold each antenna piece in half lengthwise, and whip stitch along the long edge, leaving the ends open. Cut two pipe cleaners to 10½″ long (27cm). Fold back ¼″ (5mm) of each end of the pipe cleaners. Slip one pipe cleaner into each antenna casing.

4 Attach the antennae, eye, and rickrack. Use fabric glue to attach the sliver rickrack to the bottom edge of the front of the headband. Pin and sew the antennae to the back of the headband. Use fabric glue to attach green pom-poms to the top of each antenna. Heat set the eyeball pieces back to back on each side of the headband, and whip stitch around the edges.

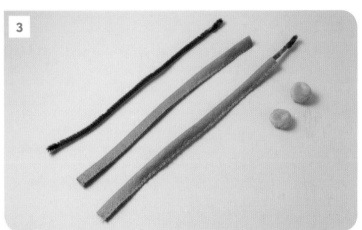

5 Measure and attach the elastic. Measure the child's head to determine the necessary length of the elastic band. Cut enough elastic to allow the headband to fit snuggly around the child's head without being too tight. Stitch the ends of the elastic band to the back of the headband.

6 Add the finishing touches. Bend the antennae into a zigzag. Stack a ¹⁹⁄₃₂″ (15mm) green glitter button on top of a ¹⁵⁄₁₆″ (25mm) black button. Stitch the buttons onto the eye to make an eyeball.

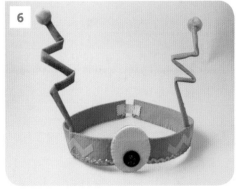

Little Boy's Alien Invasion Patterns

Enlarge patterns by 150% for actual size

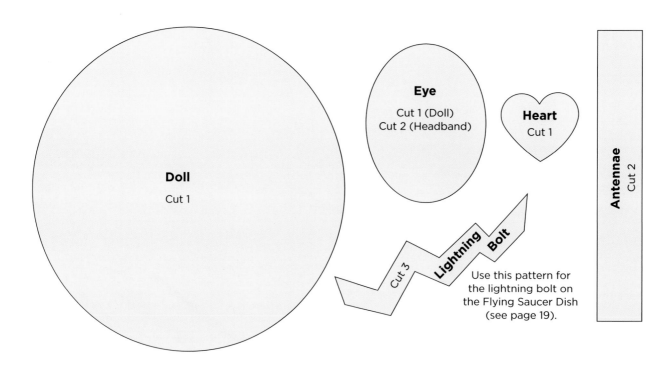

Doll

Cut 1

Eye

Cut 1 (Doll)
Cut 2 (Headband)

Heart

Cut 1

Antennae

Cut 2

Lightning Bolt

Cut 3

Use this pattern for the lightning bolt on the Flying Saucer Dish (see page 19).

Headband and Headband Antennae

Cut 2 (Headband)
Cut 1 (Headband Antennae)

Cut on fold

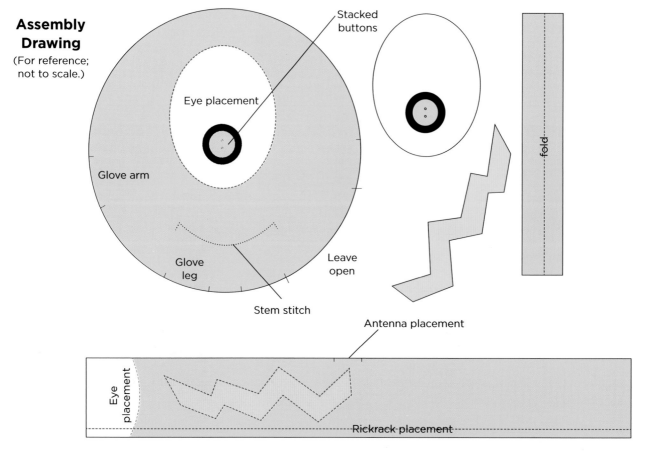

Assembly Drawing

(For reference; not to scale.)

Stacked buttons

Eye placement

Glove arm

Glove leg

Stem stitch

Leave open

fold

Antenna placement

Eye placement

Rickrack placement

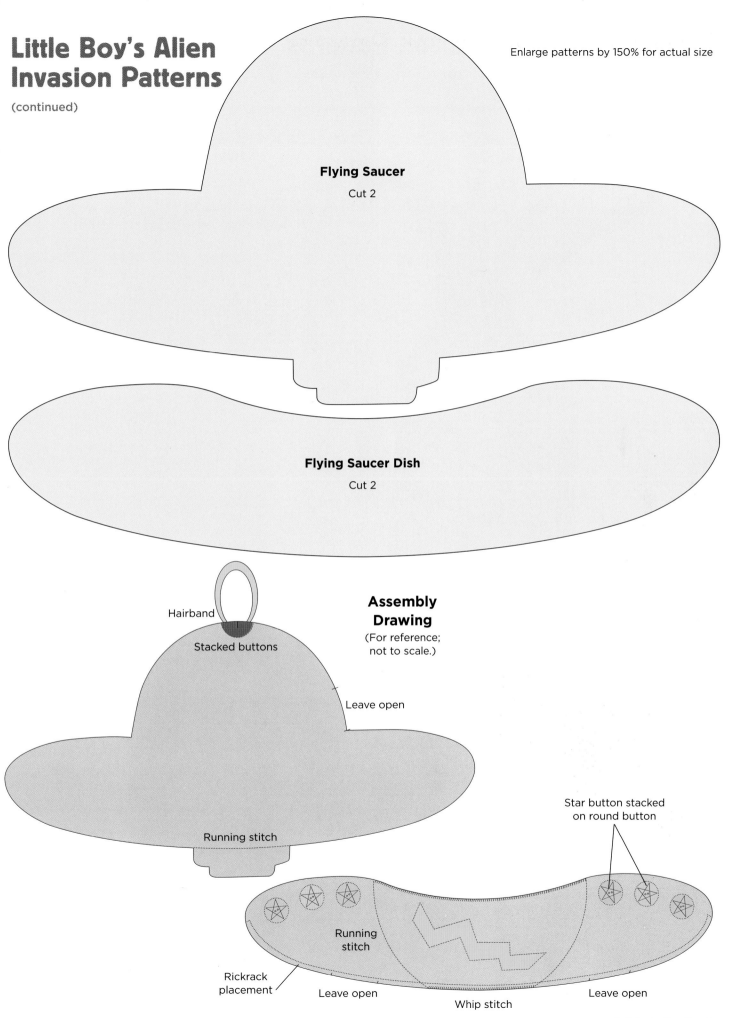

Little Boy's Alien Invasion Patterns

(continued)

Enlarge patterns by 150% for actual size

Flying Saucer

Cut 2

Flying Saucer Dish

Cut 2

Hairband

Stacked buttons

Assembly Drawing

(For reference; not to scale.)

Leave open

Running stitch

Star button stacked on round button

Running stitch

Rickrack placement

Leave open

Whip stitch

Leave open

Woodland Animal Hideout

The forest is a wonderful place to discover critters of all shapes and sizes. Here, you will find five friendly forest creatures for the little ones in your life to enjoy.

Skunk

Fluffy fur gives this skunk
an extra-soft back and tail.

Patterns on page 27.

MATERIALS AND SUPPLIES:

- Felt in black, pink, red, and white
- Embroidery thread in coordinating colors
- Embroidery needle
- One piece of 4″ (10cm)-wide fur by the yard in white
- Iron-on adhesive
- Black stretch glove
- Two ¼″ (5mm) blue buttons
- Fabric glue
- Scissors
- Fabric marker
- Pins
- Polyester fiberfill stuffing

INSTRUCTIONS:

1 Prepare the pieces. Enlarge the pattern by the required amount and cut out all the pattern pieces. From the felt, cut two black Skunks, two black Tails, two black Ears, two pink Cheeks, one pink Nose, one red Heart, and one white Chest. From the piece of white fur, cut one Forehead, one Back Stripe, and one Tail Stripe.

2 Attach the pieces. Heat set the cheeks, nose, chest, and heart. Using fabric glue, attach the forehead, back stripe, and tail stripe. Then, whip stitch along the edges of the fur pieces.

3 Add the details. Cut and stuff the black glove fingers for the arms and legs. Whip stitch around the chest, heart, cheeks, and nose. Stitch on ¼″ (5mm) blue buttons for the eyes.

4 Create the tail. Whip stitch the tail front and back pieces together, leaving an opening for stuffing. Stuff the tail and stitch the opening closed.

5 Attach the tail. Stitch the tail to the skunk's back, aligning the back and tail stripes.

6 Pin, stitch, and finish. Pin the front and back pieces together, and pin the arms, legs, and ears in place. Whip stitch the skunk together, leaving openings for stuffing. When stitching through the arms, legs, and ears, use a running stitch. Stuff the skunk and stitch the openings closed.

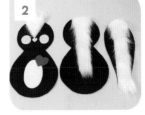

More Woodland Hideout Animals

You can use the same basic steps from the Skunk project to create four additional Woodland Hideout creatures.

Squirrel

This mischievous squirrel is always ready to play.

Patterns on page 27.

MATERIALS AND SUPPLIES:

- Felt in tan, pink, and red
- Embroidery thread in coordinating colors
- Embroidery needle
- One piece of 4″ (10cm)-wide fur by the yard in brown
- Iron-on adhesive
- Brown stretch glove
- Two ¼″ (5mm) blue buttons
- Fabric glue
- Scissors
- Fabric marker
- Pins
- Polyester fiberfill stuffing

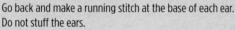

INSTRUCTIONS:

Whip stitch around the outside of the body, including the ears.

Go back and make a running stitch at the base of each ear. Do not stuff the ears.

Cut the squirrel tail slightly longer than the skunk tail as shown on the pattern. Use 4″ (10cm)-wide brown fur by the yard for the two tail pieces and the chest.

To create the tail, pin the front and back pieces right sides together, and whip stitch around the edges, leaving an opening to turn the tail right side out.

Stuff the tail and stitch the opening closed.

Stitch the tail to the back of the squirrel's body.

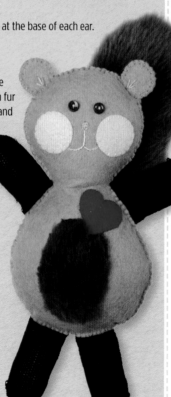

Owl

With wings that flap, and bright yellow eyes that can see through the dark, this wise owl is the perfect nighttime companion.

Patterns on page 28.

MATERIALS AND SUPPLIES:

- Felt in cream, light brown, dark brown, yellow, red, and white
- Embroidery thread in coordinating colors
- Embroidery needle
- Iron-on adhesive
- Cream stretch glove
- Two ¾″ (20mm) yellow glitter buttons
- Eight ¼″ (5mm) brown buttons
- Four ½″ (15mm) brown buttons
- Scissors
- Fabric marker
- Pins
- Polyester fiberfill stuffing

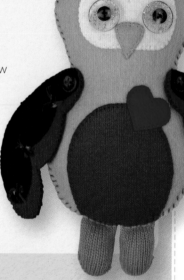

INSTRUCTIONS:

Cut two glove fingers 1½″ (4cm) long for the owl's feet.

Heat set an upper wing on each wing base, lining them up along the outer edges. Be sure to create the wings so you have a left and right wing.

Whip stitch around the edges of all the felt pieces except the body. Then, whip stitch around the edges of the body pieces, leaving openings for stuffing.

Place a ½″ (15mm) button at the top of the wing, and another ½″ (15mm) button at the back of the body. Hold the wing in place and stitch through the top button, wing, body, and back button. Stitch three times through the wing and body layers. This will allow the wing to move from side to side.

Bunny Rabbit

A sweet white bunny will make any child smile!

Patterns on page 29.

MATERIALS AND SUPPLIES:

- Felt in white, pink, and red
- Embroidery thread in coordinating colors
- Embroidery needle
- Iron-on adhesive
- White stretch glove
- Two ¼" (5mm) blue buttons
- 1 white 1½" (4cm) pom-pom or small pom-pom maker
- 1 pipe cleaner
- Fabric glue
- Scissors
- Permanent marker
- Pins
- Polyester fiberfill stuffing

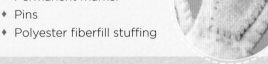

INSTRUCTIONS:

Heat set the bunny's inner ear pieces to the front body piece, and whip stitch around the inner ear pieces.

On the back side of the front body piece, fabric glue a 2½" (6.5cm)-long pipe cleaner to the back of each ear.

Whip stitch the front and back body pieces together, stitching around the outside of the body, including the ears.

Go back to the ears and make a running stitch at the base of each ear. Do not stuff the ears.

After the stitching and stuffing is done, glue or stitch a pom-pom tail to the back of the bunny's body. You can make your own pom-pom with a pom-pom maker like the one produced by Clover.

Frog

This smiling frog is always happy to see you.

Patterns on page 29.

MATERIALS AND SUPPLIES:

- Felt in green, red, pink, and white
- Embroidery thread in coordinating colors
- Embroidery needle
- Iron-on adhesive
- Green stretch glove
- Two ½" (15mm) black buttons
- Scissors
- Permanent marker
- Pins
- Polyester fiberfill stuffing

INSTRUCTIONS:

Heat set the eyes, mouth, tongue, and heart.

Whip stitch around the eyes and heart; back stitch around the mouth and tongue; use a long back stitch to create the nose; and blanket stitch around the body.

Use ½" (15mm) black buttons for the pupils.

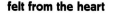

Woodland Hideout Tree House

The Woodland Hideout Tree House is made with a two-liter plastic bottle, and is complete with a front door and window! You can store one or two Woodland Hideout animals in the tree house. Super cute!

Patterns on page 30–31.

MATERIALS AND SUPPLIES:

- Felt in dark brown, medium brown, light brown, chartreuse, green, moss, white, light red, and gray-brown
- Embroidery thread in coordinating colors
- Embroidery needle
- Iron-on adhesive
- 1 plastic two-liter bottle
- 5 pipe cleaners
- Thirty-one ¼" (5mm) green buttons
- Scissors
- Wire cutters
- Permanent marker
- Pins
- Polyester fiberfill stuffing

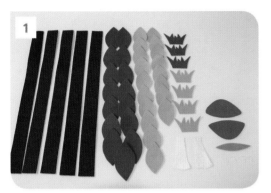

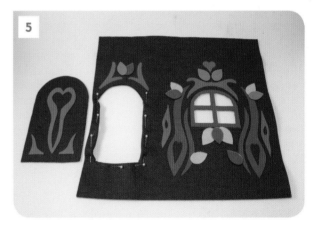

INSTRUCTIONS:

1 Prepare the first set of pieces. Enlarge the pattern by the required amount and cut out all the pattern pieces. From the felt, cut five dark brown Tree House Branches, sixteen chartreuse #4 Leaves, sixteen green #3 Leaves, four chartreuse Grasses, three moss Grasses, two white Mushroom Stems, two light red Mushroom Tops, one gray-brown Mushroom Underside, and four white mushroom dots.

2 Prepare the second set of pieces. Cut the following pieces from felt, and attach iron-on adhesive to the back of each one: two each medium brown Wood Grain #1 and #2, two light brown Wood Grain #3, one medium brown Window Frame, one light brown Window Branch, one light brown Over Window Heart, four chartreuse, four green, and three moss #1 leaves, and two moss #2 leaves.

3 Prepare the base. Using the pattern piece, cut one Tree Base from brown felt. Following the pattern, cut and fold the door opening and mark the placement of the window. Also cut the Bottom Cover.

4 Prepare the door pieces. For the door, use the pattern to cut two dark brown felt Doors. Cut the following additional door pieces from felt and attach iron-on adhesive to the back of each one: one light brown Door Wood Grain piece, two light brown Over Door Branches, two light brown Door Sides, three chartreuse and one green #1 leaves, and three moss #2 leaves.

5 Attach the window and door pieces. Heat set all the window and door pieces onto the tree house base as shown. Cut away the felt inside the windowpanes. Pin under ½" (15mm) of felt on the sides and bottom of the door opening and press.

6 Add the details to the door. Whip stitch around all wood grain pieces on the door front. Blanket stitch the front and back door pieces together, leaving the bottom open. Heat set the leaves as shown, placing one set on the front of the door and a matching set on back. Using the pattern, cut the plastic door insert.

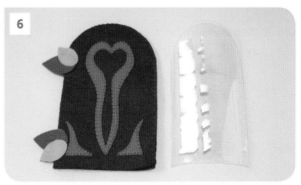

(Continued on following page)

7 Finish the door. Slip the liter bottle door insert into the felt door. Blanket stitch the bottom of the door closed.

8 Add the details to the tree house base. Use whip and back stitches to embroider the pieces on the tree house base. For the mushroom, stem stitch the mouth on one of the top pieces and use French knots for eyes. Heat set the mushroom dots onto the mushroom top, and trim as needed. Heat set the mushroom underside to the mushroom top. Whip stitch around the dots and underside pieces. Pin the stem pieces in place, one on the front and one on the back of the mushroom. Whip stitch around the entire mushroom, leaving a small opening for stuffing. Lightly stuff the mushroom, and whip stitch the opening closed. Stitch the mushroom to the tree house base as shown. Note: If you're short on time, simply heat set the pieces in place and skip the embroidery. You can always go back and add embroidery stitches later.

9 Shape the tree house. Bring the edges of the tree house base together and pin them. Whip stitch the edges so you have a tube. Pin the bottom cover to the bottom end of the tree house, and whip stitch them together. Slip the liter bottle into the tree house from the top. Attach the front door by stitching the leaf hinges to the side of the door opening.

10 Create the branches. Fold each branch piece in half, and whip stitch along the long edges. Cut the pipe cleaners to 10½" (27cm). Fold back ¼" (5mm) of each end of the pipe cleaners. Slip one pipe cleaner into the branch casing. Gather the branches together, and fold or twist a few to make bent, short branches. Wrap thread around the branches to hold them together. Then, stitch through all of the branches. To attach the leaves, pinch the bottom point of a leaf and place a ¼" (5mm) green button against the folded felt. Stitch through the button, the pinched leaf, a branch, and through another leaf or button on the opposite side of the branch. How you place your leaves and bend the branches is up to you.

11 Finish the tree house. Half an inch (15mm) from the top edge of the tree house, make a running base stitch, and gather the felt around the top of the bottle. Push the bundle of tree branches into the top of the bottle.

Woodland Animal Hideout Patterns

Enlarge patterns by 135% for actual size

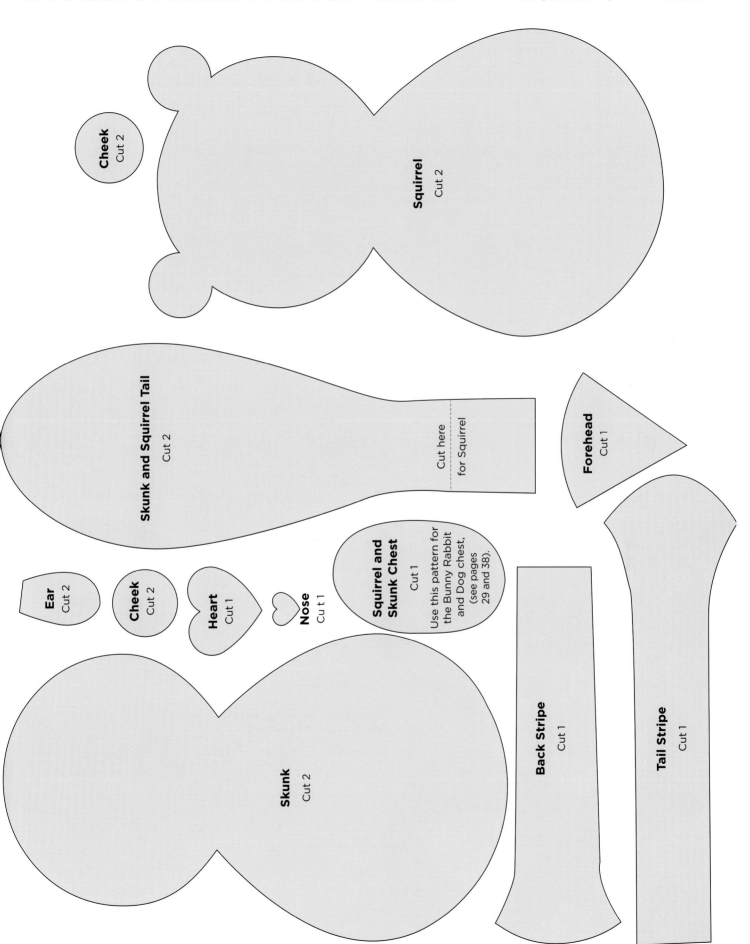

Cheek Cut 2

Squirrel Cut 2

Skunk and Squirrel Tail Cut 2

Cut here for Squirrel

Forehead Cut 1

Ear Cut 2

Cheek Cut 2

Heart Cut 1

Nose Cut 1

Squirrel and Skunk Chest Cut 1

Use this pattern for the Bunny Rabbit and Dog chest, (see pages 29 and 38).

Skunk Cut 2

Back Stripe Cut 1

Tail Stripe Cut 1

Woodland Animal Hideout Patterns (continued)

Enlarge patterns by 135% for actual size

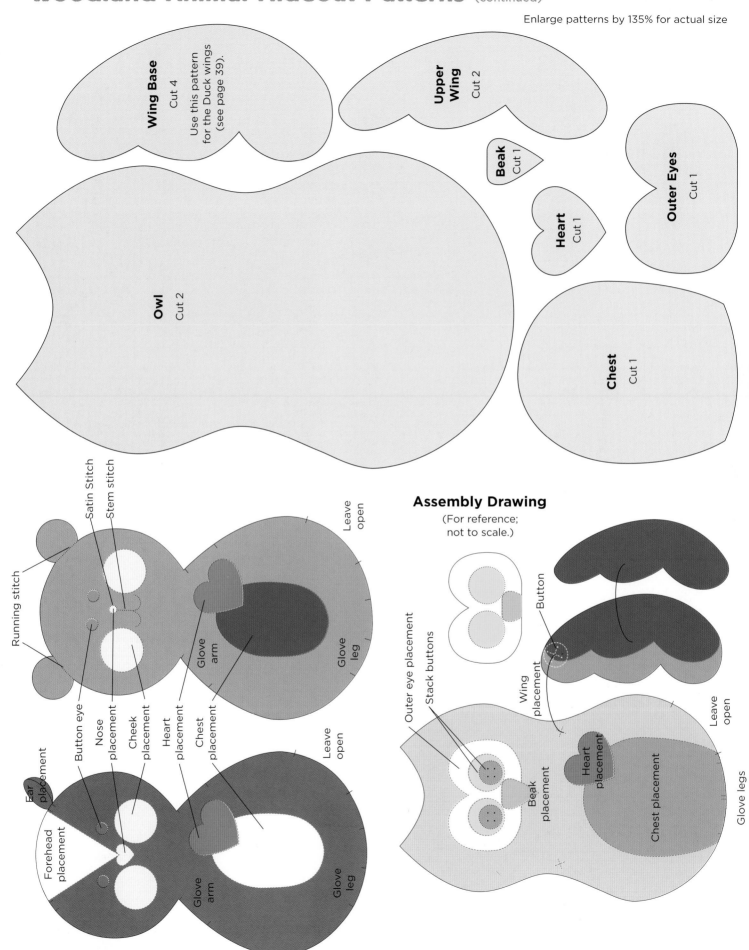

Wing Base
Cut 4

Use this pattern for the Duck wings (see page 39).

Upper Wing
Cut 2

Beak
Cut 1

Heart
Cut 1

Outer Eyes
Cut 1

Owl
Cut 2

Chest
Cut 1

Satin Stitch
Stem stitch
Running stitch
Leave open
Glove arm
Glove leg
Ear placement
Forehead placement
Button eye
Nose placement
Cheek placement
Heart placement
Chest placement
Glove arm
Glove leg
Leave open

Assembly Drawing
(For reference; not to scale.)

Button
Outer eye placement
Stack buttons
Wing placement
Beak placement
Heart placement
Chest placement
Leave open
Glove legs

Woodland Animal Hideout Patterns (continued)

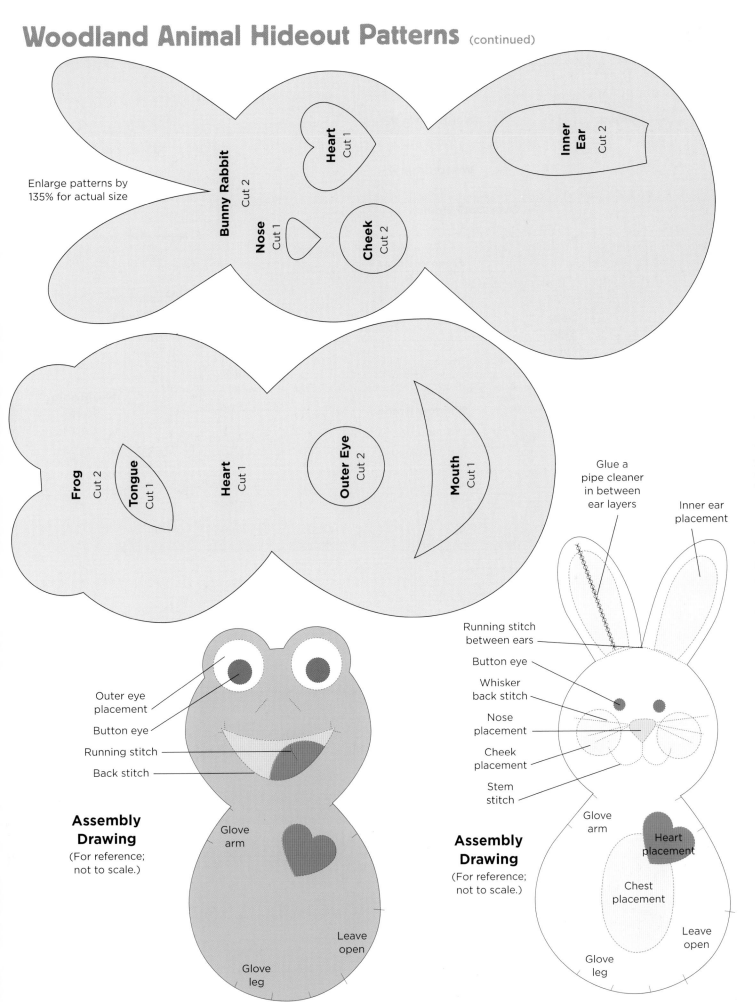

Enlarge patterns by 135% for actual size

Bunny Rabbit
Cut 2

Heart
Cut 1

Inner Ear
Cut 2

Nose
Cut 1

Cheek
Cut 2

Frog
Cut 2

Tongue
Cut 1

Heart
Cut 1

Outer Eye
Cut 2

Mouth
Cut 1

Outer eye placement
Button eye
Running stitch
Back stitch

Assembly Drawing
(For reference; not to scale.)

Glove arm

Leave open

Glove leg

Glue a pipe cleaner in between ear layers

Inner ear placement

Running stitch between ears

Button eye

Whisker back stitch

Nose placement

Cheek placement

Stem stitch

Glove arm

Heart placement

Chest placement

Leave open

Glove leg

Assembly Drawing
(For reference; not to scale.)

Woodland Animal Hideout Patterns (continued)

Enlarge patterns on this page
by 160% for actual size

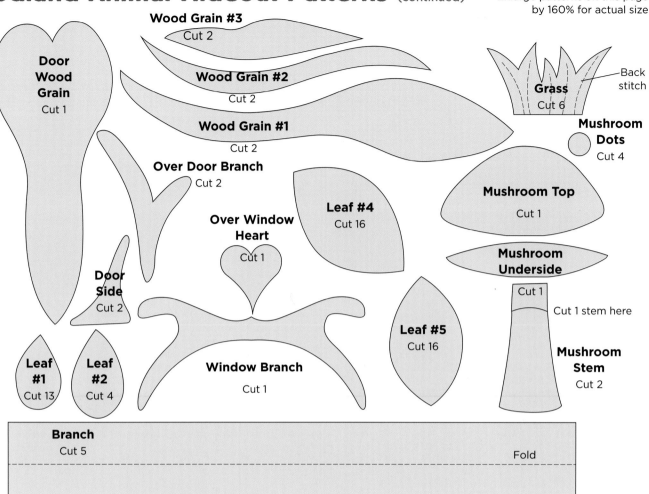

Wood Grain #3
Cut 2

Wood Grain #2
Cut 2

Wood Grain #1
Cut 2

Door Wood Grain
Cut 1

Over Door Branch
Cut 2

Over Window Heart
Cut 1

Leaf #4
Cut 16

Door Side
Cut 2

Window Branch
Cut 1

Leaf #5
Cut 16

Leaf #1
Cut 13

Leaf #2
Cut 4

Grass
Cut 6

Back stitch

Mushroom Dots
Cut 4

Mushroom Top
Cut 1

Mushroom Underside
Cut 1

Cut 1 stem here

Mushroom Stem
Cut 2

Branch
Cut 5

Fold

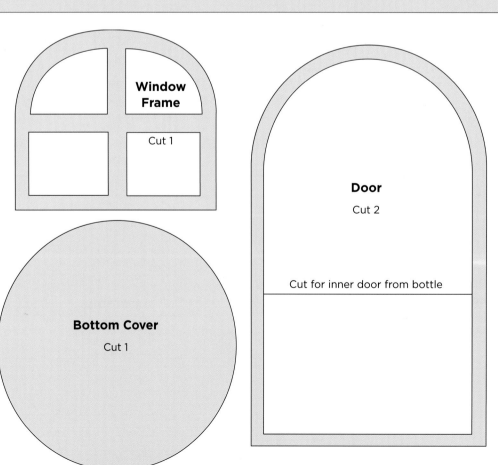

Window Frame
Cut 1

Door
Cut 2

Cut for inner door from bottle

Bottom Cover
Cut 1

Woodland Animal Hideout Patterns (continued)

Enlarge patterns by 225% for actual size

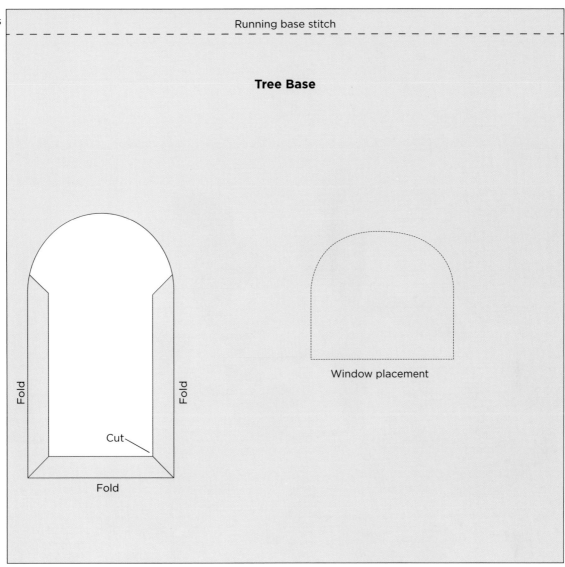

Running base stitch

Tree Base

Fold

Fold

Cut

Fold

Window placement

Assembly Drawing

(For reference; not to scale.)

Button

Eyelet

Barnyard Bonanza

Lots of fun animals can be found on the farm, each with their own fun personalities. Here, you will learn how to make some well-known barnyard favorites, including a cat, a cow, and a pig.

Barnyard Bonanza Cat

This friendly feline is bound to be your
little one's new favorite toy!

Patterns on page 38.

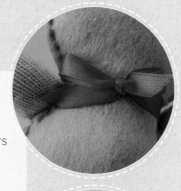

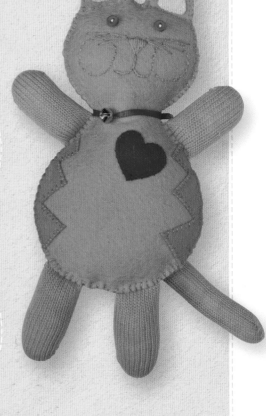

MATERIALS AND SUPPLIES:

- Felt in golden yellow, gray, pink, and red
- Embroidery thread in coordinating colors
- Embroidery needle
- Cream stretch glove
- Iron-on adhesive
- Two ¼" (5mm) blue buttons
- Red ribbon
- 1 small jingle bell
- Scissors
- Permanent marker
- Pins
- Polyester fiberfill stuffing

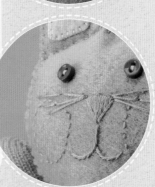

INSTRUCTIONS:

1 Prepare the first set of pieces. Enlarge the pattern by the required amount and
cut out all the pattern pieces. From the felt, cut two golden yellow Cats, two gray
Stripes, two pink Inner Ears, and one red Heart. Cut three fingers and the thumb off
the glove. Trace the Tail pattern on the glove's pinky. Stitch along the pattern lines
before cutting the tail out. Mark the face details on the felt.

2 Add the details. Heat set the inner ears, heart, and stripes. Embroider the cat's
face as indicated on the pattern. Whip stitch around the edges of the inner ears,
satin stitch the nose, use long back stitches for the whiskers, stem stitch the mouth,
and use running stitches for the cheeks. Stitch on ¼" (5mm) blue buttons for eyes.
Stuff the arms, legs, and tail.

3 Pin. Pin the front and back body pieces together. Pin the arms and legs in place.

4 Stitch, stuff, and finish. Whip stitch the cat together, leaving an opening for
stuffing. When stitching through the ears, arms, and legs, use a running stitch. Add
stuffing and stitch the opening closed. Stitch the tail to the back. Tie red ribbon with
a small jingle bell attached around the neck for a collar.

More Barnyard Bonanza Animals

You can use the same basic steps from the Cat project to create four additional Barnyard Bonanza creatures.

Dog

In this barnyard, dogs and cats get along. So once he is made, this dog will be ready to play with any of the barnyard animals.

Patterns on page 38.

MATERIALS AND SUPPLIES:

- Felt in light brown, chocolate brown, dark brown, black, and red
- Embroidery thread in coordinating colors
- Embroidery needle
- Iron-on adhesive
- Dark brown stretch glove
- Two ¼" (5mm) blue buttons
- Two ½" (15mm) black buttons
- Four ½" (15mm) brown buttons
- Scissors
- Permanent marker
- Pins
- Polyester fiberfill stuffing

INSTRUCTIONS:

Heat set all appliqué pieces as shown on the pattern and whip stitch around the edges.

Stem stitch the mouth.

Stack two ¼" (5mm) blue buttons over two ½" (15mm) black buttons for the eyes and stitch them in place.

For the ears, heat set the ear backs to the ear fronts, lining them up along the outside edges. Be sure to make a left ear and a right ear. Whip stitch around the edges.

Place a ½" (15mm) brown button on the base of each ear, and stitch through the button, the ear, the dog's body, and through another ½" (15mm) button positioned on the back side of the dog. Stitch three times through all the ear layers. This will allow the ear to move from side to side.

Trace the dog tail pattern onto the pinky of the stretch glove, and stitch along the pattern lines before cutting it out. Stitch the tail to the back.

Cow

This cow has her own cowbell to let you know when it's playtime!

Patterns on page 40.

MATERIALS AND SUPPLIES:

- Felt in white, black, tan, pink, and red
- Embroidery thread in coordinating colors
- Embroidery needle
- Iron-on adhesive
- Black stretch glove
- Two ⅝" (15mm) brown buttons
- Two ½" (15mm) blue glitter buttons
- Black yarn
- Red ribbon
- Miniature cowbell
- Scissors
- Permanent marker
- Pins
- Polyester fiberfill stuffing

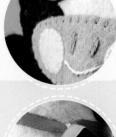

INSTRUCTIONS:

From the felt, cut two white Cows, two black Face Spots, one black Left Spot, one black Right Spot, two black Ears, one tan Snout, two pink Cheeks, two black Ears, and one red Heart.

Heat set the snout, cheeks, spots, and heart.

Whip stitch around the edges of all the appliqué pieces. For the spots, only whip stitch along the inside edges.

Stem stitch the mouth and satin stitch the nostrils.

Eyelash stitch the eyelashes. Then, stack the brown and blue glitter buttons for the eyes, and stitch them in place.

Pin together the body, ears, legs, and arms. Whip stitch around the body, leaving an opening for stuffing.

Stuff the cow and stitch the opening closed.

Braid black yarn to make a tail, and stitch it to the back of the cow.

Pig

No barnyard would be complete without a perfectly pink pig!

Patterns on page 39.

MATERIALS AND SUPPLIES:

- Felt in pink, light pink, gray, and red
- Embroidery thread in coordinating colors
- Embroidery needle
- Iron-on adhesive
- Pink stretch glove
- Two ¼" (5mm) blue buttons
- 1 pipe cleaner
- Wire cutters
- Scissors
- Permanent marker
- Pins
- Polyester fiberfill stuffing

INSTRUCTIONS:

Heat set the inner ears, snout, nose pieces, and heart.

Stem stitch mouth, and whip stitch around all the appliqué pieces.

Stitch two ¼" (5mm) blue buttons in place for the eyes.

Pin together the body pieces, and pin the legs and arms in place. Whip stitch around the body, leaving an opening for stuffing. When stitching through the ears, arms, and legs, use a running stitch.

Stuff the pig and stitch the opening closed.

For the tail, fold the tail piece in half lengthwise, and whip stitch along the long edge, leaving ends open.

Cut a pipe cleaner to 5" (13cm)

Fold back ¼" (5mm) of each end of the pipe cleaner.

Slip the pipe cleaner into the tail casing, and stitch both ends closed.

Curl the tail around a pencil and stitch it to the back of the pig.

Duck

This yellow fellow's cheerful color is sure to brighten up your day.

Patterns on page 39.

MATERIALS AND SUPPLIES:

- Felt in light yellow, dark yellow, pink, orange, and red
- Embroidery thread in coordinating colors
- Embroidery needle
- Iron-on adhesive
- Yellow stretch glove
- Two ½" (15mm) blue glitter buttons
- Four ½" (15mm) yellow buttons
- Orange yarn
- Scissors
- Permanent marker
- Pins
- Polyester fiberfill stuffing

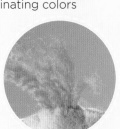

INSTRUCTIONS:

Use two fingers cut from a stretch glove for the legs.

Heat set the cheeks and heart, and whip stitch around the edges of these pieces.

Fold duck bill in half and stitch ¼" (5mm) along each side. Pin the bill to the face so it overlaps the cheeks, and stitch it in place.

Loop orange yarn at the top of the duck's head, and pin it in place.

Pin body pieces together, and pin the legs in place. Whip stitch the body together, leaving an opening for stuffing. Stuff the duck and stitch the opening closed.

Heat set the wings together in pairs, lining them up along the outside edges. Be sure to create the wings so you have a left and right wing.

Whip stitch around the edges of the wings.

Place a ½" (15mm) button at the top of the wing, and another ½" (15mm) button at the back of the body. Hold the wing in place and stitch through the top button, wing, body, and back button. Stitch three times through the wing and body layers. This will allow the wing to move from side to side.

Barnyard Bonanza
Barnyard Roll-Up

This project uses a bandana to make an adorable barnyard fence with pockets to hold all your barnyard bonanza friends.

Patterns on page 40.

MATERIALS AND SUPPLIES:

* Felt in white, green, and yellow
* Embroidery thread in coordinating colors
* Embroidery needle
* Iron-on adhesive
* 1 full-size red bandanna
* Red ribbon
* Five ½" (15mm) red buttons
* Scissors
* Permanent marker
* Pins

INSTRUCTIONS:

1 Prepare the bandanna. Open and press the full-size red bandanna. Lay the bandanna wrong side up. Pin along the center.

2 Fold the in edges. Bring the bottom and top of the bandanna together in the center, and pin them in place.

3 Fold and pin the pockets. Fold the bandanna in half so that the pinned edges are on the outside. Pin approximately every 5½" (14cm) along the top and bottom. This will create back-to-back pockets after stitching.

4 Stitch the pockets and ribbon. Mark the location of the pockets by lightly drawing a line between the pins along the top and bottom edges. Using a close running stitch, stitch along these lines. Then, cut a 40" (100cm)-long piece of red ¼" (5mm) ribbon. Fold the ribbon in half, and pin it to the right edge of the bandanna, between the folded layers. Whip stitch the right and left sides of the bandanna together, stitching through the ribbon on the right side. This will create eight pockets.

5 Prepare the felt pieces. Cut and attach iron-on adhesive to the following pieces: four white Top/Bottom pieces, ten white Fence Posts, sixteen white Cross Planks, five green Grasses, and five yellow Flowers.

6 Attach the fence pieces. Heat set the fence pieces as shown. Attach the top and bottom pieces along the top and bottom of the bandanna. Attach the cross planks in an X pattern, and then add the posts. Repeat on the other side of the bandanna.

7 Add the details and finish. Heat set the grass and flower pieces, trimming the edges of the outer grass pieces as shown on the pattern. Embroider these pieces if desired. If you do so, be careful not to stitch through the pockets. Stitch ½" (15mm) red glitter buttons in the center of each flower.

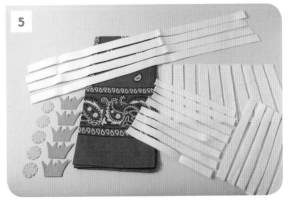

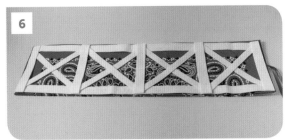

Barnyard Bonanza Patterns

Enlarge patterns by 150% for actual size

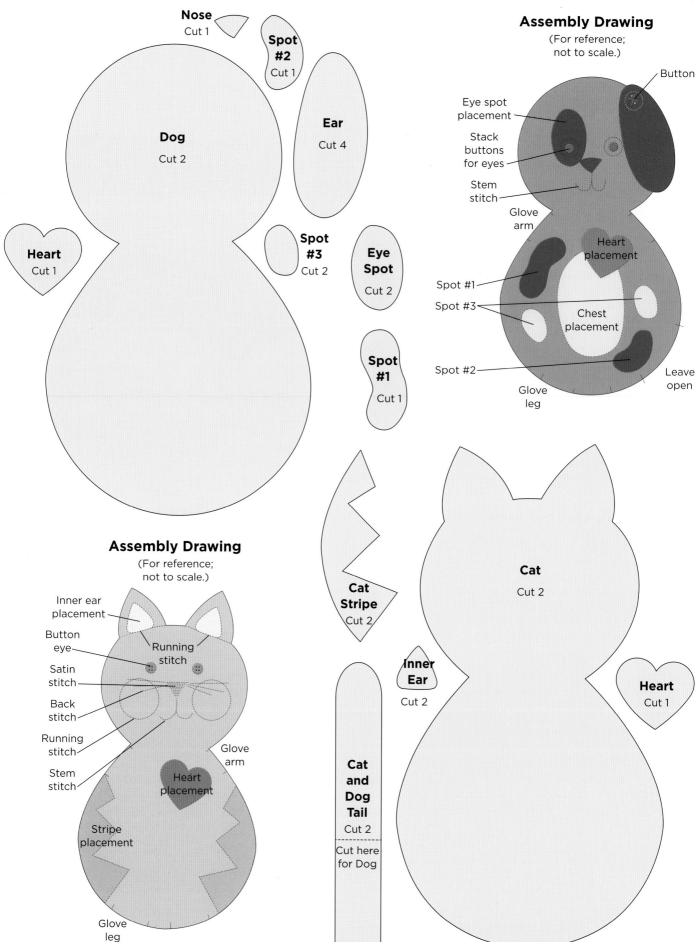

Nose
Cut 1

Spot #2
Cut 1

Ear
Cut 4

Dog
Cut 2

Heart
Cut 1

Spot #3
Cut 2

Eye Spot
Cut 2

Spot #1
Cut 1

Assembly Drawing
(For reference; not to scale.)

Button

Eye spot placement

Stack buttons for eyes

Stem stitch

Glove arm

Heart placement

Spot #1

Spot #3

Chest placement

Spot #2

Glove leg

Leave open

Assembly Drawing
(For reference; not to scale.)

Inner ear placement

Button eye

Running stitch

Satin stitch

Back stitch

Running stitch

Stem stitch

Glove arm

Heart placement

Stripe placement

Glove leg

Cat Stripe
Cut 2

Cat
Cut 2

Inner Ear
Cut 2

Heart
Cut 1

Cat and Dog Tail
Cut 2

Cut here for Dog

Barnyard Bonanza Patterns (continued)

Enlarge patterns by 150% for actual size

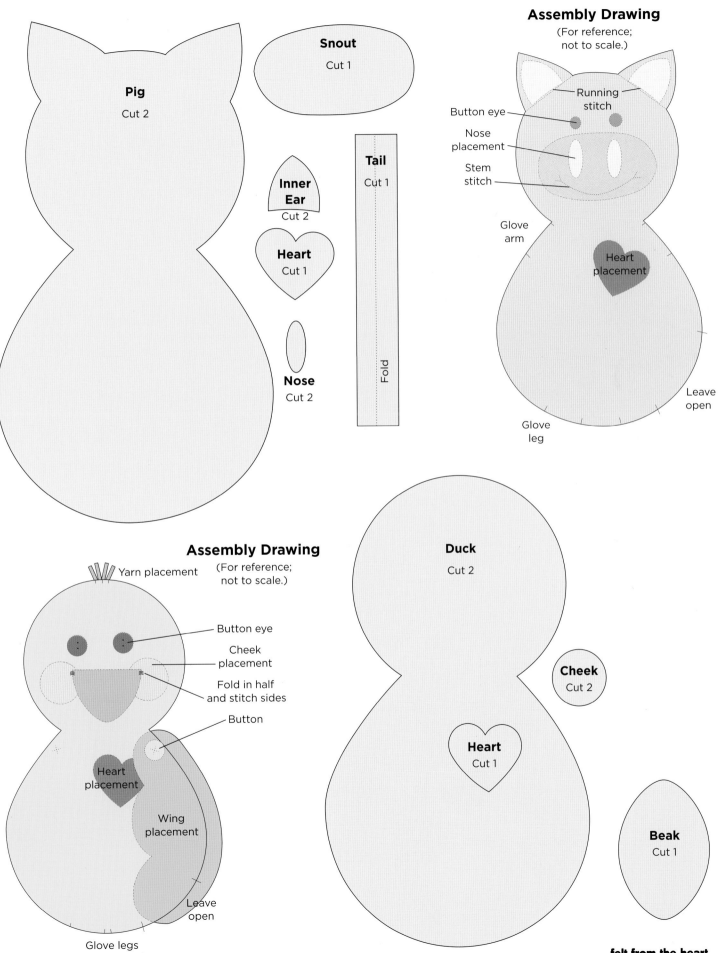

Pig
Cut 2

Snout
Cut 1

Inner Ear
Cut 2

Tail
Cut 1

Fold

Heart
Cut 1

Nose
Cut 2

Assembly Drawing
(For reference; not to scale.)

Running stitch

Button eye

Nose placement

Stem stitch

Glove arm

Heart placement

Glove leg

Leave open

Assembly Drawing
(For reference; not to scale.)

Yarn placement

Button eye

Cheek placement

Fold in half and stitch sides

Button

Heart placement

Wing placement

Leave open

Glove legs

Duck
Cut 2

Cheek
Cut 2

Heart
Cut 1

Beak
Cut 1

Barnyard Bonanza Patterns (continued)

Enlarge patterns by 150% for actual size

Enlarge patterns by 150% for actual size

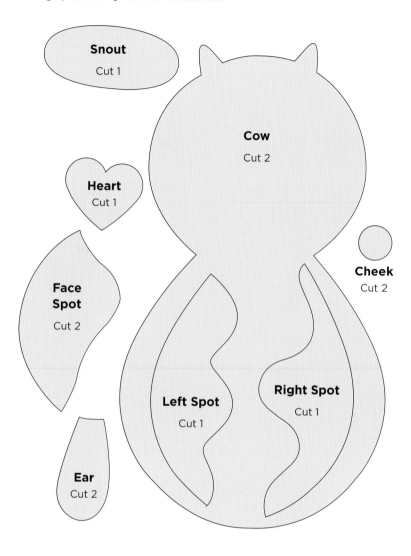

Snout
Cut 1

Cow
Cut 2

Heart
Cut 1

Cheek
Cut 2

Face
Spot
Cut 2

Left Spot
Cut 1

Right Spot
Cut 1

Ear
Cut 2

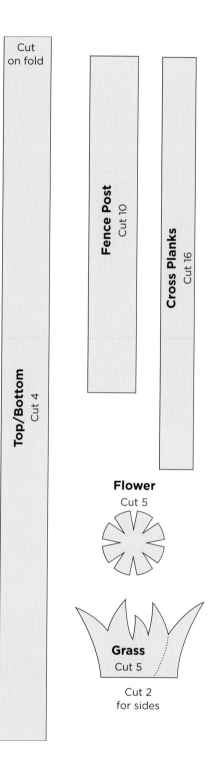

Cut
on fold

Top/Bottom
Cut 4

Fence Post
Cut 10

Cross Planks
Cut 16

Flower
Cut 5

Grass
Cut 5

Cut 2
for sides

Assembly Drawing

(For reference;
not to scale.)

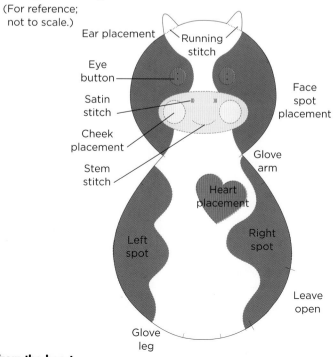

Ear placement

Running
stitch

Eye
button

Satin
stitch

Cheek
placement

Stem
stitch

Face
spot
placement

Glove
arm

Heart
placement

Left
spot

Right
spot

Leave
open

Glove
leg

My Secret Garden

Every little boy and girl needs lots of fruits and vegetable to grow up healthy and strong, but green things aren't always their dinnertime favorites. Change their minds with this collection of nutritious garden critters!

Apple & Worm

Apples are a crunchy sweet fruit that can be used to make all kinds of goodies, from cider to pie. But look out—this apple has a worm!

Patterns on page 46.

MATERIALS AND SUPPLIES:

- ◆ Felt in red, light red, green, chartreuse, and brown
- ◆ Embroidery thread in coordinating colors
- ◆ Embroidery needle
- ◆ Iron-on adhesive
- ◆ Red stretch glove
- ◆ 1 pipe cleaner
- ◆ Scissors
- ◆ Permanent marker
- ◆ Pins
- ◆ Polyester fiberfill stuffing

INSTRUCTIONS:

1 Prepare the pieces. Enlarge the pattern by the required amount and cut out all the pattern pieces. From the felt, cut two red Apples, two chartreuse Worms, one green Leaf, one light red Heart, and one brown Stem.

2 Prepare the apple. Using the pattern as a reference, cut a hole from one of the apple pieces. Heat set the heart. Cut one finger from the glove.

3 Pin the finger. Pin the finger from the glove to the hole on the back side of the apple.

4 Attach the finger. Whip stitch around the finger, catching the edge of the hole in the apple. Push the finger through to the back side of the apple piece. The finger will now be inside out and the stitched edge will be hidden. Whip stitch around the edges of the heart.

5 Stitch the leaf, stem, and apple. Back stitch down the center of the leaf. Then, make a running base stitch ⅛″ (5mm) from the edges, and pull the thread to lightly gather the leaf. Fold the stem in half, and whip stitch along the long edge. Pin the stem and leaf in place. Pin the edge of the glove finger to the apple bottom. Whip stitch around the edges of the two apple pieces, being sure to catch the glove finger in the stitches and leave an opening for stuffing. Stuff the apple and stitch the opening closed.

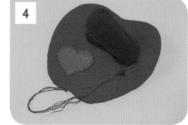

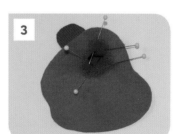

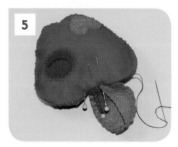

6 Create the worm. Stem stitch the worm's mouth on the top worm piece, and use French knots for eyes. Pin the two worm pieces together, and blanket stitch around the edges, changing the stitch size as you go. Leave the worm's head open. Fold a pipe cleaner in half and push it into the worm's body. Add stuffing to the head, and stitch closed.

More Secret Garden Characters

You can use the same basic steps from the Apple & Worm project to create four additional My Secret Garden characters.

Three Peas in a Pod

Who knew peas could be so cute? These three little guys can be tucked away safely into their pod when playtime is over.

Patterns on page 47.

MATERIALS AND SUPPLIES:

- Felt in chartreuse, green, red, and pink
- Embroidery thread in coordinating colors
- Embroidery needle
- Iron-on adhesive
- 1 green hairband
- One ¼" (5mm) green button
- Two ½" (15mm) green glitter buttons
- Scissors
- Permanent marker
- Pins
- Polyester fiberfill stuffing

INSTRUCTIONS:

Create the peas by cutting the necessary pieces from felt, heat setting the cheeks, and embroidering the mouths. Heat set a heart on the back of each pea.

Blanket stitch around the edges of the peas and leave an opening for stuffing. Stuff the peas and stitch the opening closed.

For the pod, cut three pod pieces from green felt and one red heart.

Fold two of the pod pieces in half, and press them.

Place the two folded pod pieces on the third piece, positioning the folds facing center. Pin around the outside edges, and then blanket stitch around the edges. Heat set the heart in place.

Lift up the right flap of the pod and stitch a hairband with a ¼" (5mm) button positioned in the center in place.

Lift up the left flap of the pod and stitch two ½" (15mm) green glitter buttons in place.

Place the peas in the pod, and close the pod by securing the hairband over the buttons.

Broccoli

The heartfelt smile on this green veggie is sure to make him a favorite.

Patterns on page 46.

MATERIALS AND SUPPLIES:

- Felt in chartreuse, pink, and red
- Embroidery thread in coordinating colors
- Embroidery needle
- Iron-on adhesive
- Two ¼" (5mm) green buttons
- ½" (15mm) green pom-poms
- Scissors
- Fabric glue
- Permanent marker
- Pins
- Polyester fiberfill stuffing

INSTRUCTIONS:

Cut the required pieces from felt, and heat set the cheeks and heart. Embroider the mouth, and use an eyelash stitch for the eyelashes. Stitch ¼" (5mm) green buttons in place for the eyes.

Pin the two broccoli pieces together, and whip stitch around the edges, leaving an opening for stuffing. Stuff the broccoli and stitch the opening closed.

For the broccoli top, use fabric glue to attach ½" (15mm) green pom-poms as shown.

Carrot

This cuddly carrot has his own customizable hairdo!

Patterns on page 46.

MATERIALS AND SUPPLIES:

- Felt in orange, dark green, pink, and red
- Embroidery thread in coordinating colors
- Embroidery needle
- Iron-on adhesive
- Two ¼" (5mm) green buttons
- Scissors
- Permanent marker
- Pins
- Polyester fiberfill stuffing

INSTRUCTIONS:

Cut the required pieces from felt, and heat set the cheeks and heart. Embroider the mouth, and use an eyelash stitch for the eyelashes. Stitch ¼" (5mm) green buttons in place for the eyes. Back stitch accent lines near the tip of the carrot.

Fold the carrot tops in half, making loops. Wrap and stitch around and through each loop 1" (2.5cm) from the bottom.

Make a running base stitch ¼" (5mm) from the top edge of he carrot.

Stuff the carrot, add the carrot top, and stitch closed.

Butterfly

Every garden needs a colorful butterfly to visit all the growing plants.

Patterns on page 48.

MATERIALS AND SUPPLIES:

- Felt in yellow, orange, red, and black
- Embroidery thread in coordinating colors
- Embroidery needle
- Iron-on adhesive
- 2 pipe cleaners
- 1 yellow hairband
- Two ¾" (20mm) red glitter buttons
- Two ¾" (20mm) yellow glitter buttons
- Two ½" (15mm) red glitter buttons
- Two ½" (15mm) yellow glitter buttons
- Scissors
- Wire cutters
- Permanent marker
- Pins
- Polyester fiberfill stuffing

INSTRUCTIONS:

Heat set the hearts as shown on the pattern, and whip stitch around edges. Stitch ½" (15mm) and ¾" (20mm) yellow and red glitter buttons in place.

Pin the wings together, and whip stitch around edges, leaving two openings for stuffing.

Fold the antenna piece in half lengthwise, and whip stitch along the long edge.

Cut two pipe cleaners to 4½" (11.5cm) in length. Fold back ¼" (5mm) of each end of one pipe cleaner, and slip the pipe cleaner into the antenna casing.

On the front body piece, stem stitch the mouth and use French knots for eyes. Pin the body front and back pieces in place over the wings.

Fold the antenna piece in half, and pin it between the layers of the head. Whip stitch around the edges of the head, and use a running stitch around the edges of the body on the wings. Be sure to stitch through the front and back body pieces.

Leave the point at the bottom of the body open. Fold back ¼" (5mm) of each end of the remaining pipe cleaner, and push it into the body. Stitch the body closed.

Lightly stuff the wings. Add a hairband to the upper right side, and stitch the wings closed.

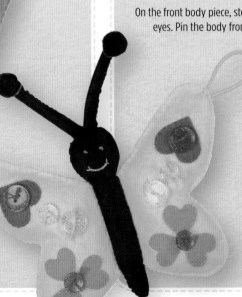

My Secret Garden Clay Pot

This clay pot provides a place for any garden critter to grow.

Patterns on page 48.

MATERIALS AND SUPPLIES:

- Felt in reddish brown and dark brown
- Embroidery thread in coordinating colors
- Embroidery needle
- Iron-on adhesive
- 1.5 liter plastic bottle
- Scissors
- Fabric glue
- Permanent marker

INSTRUCTIONS:

1 Prepare the pieces. Enlarge the pattern by the required amount and cut out all the pattern pieces. From the felt, cut one reddish brown Clay Pot, two reddish brown Edges, one reddish brown Dirt Base, one reddish brown Pot Bottom, one dark brown Dirt Center, and one dark brown Heart.

2 Heat set the necessary items. Heat set the two clay pot edges to the top of the clay pot base, and whip stitch around the edges. Do the same with the heart. Heat set the dirt center on the dirt base. Cut through both layers of felt as shown on pattern, and blanket stitch around the cut X layers.

3 Prepare the pot. Bring the edges of the clay pot together and pin them. Whip stitch the edges so you have a tube. Make a running base stitch ¼" (5mm) from the bottom edge of the clay pot base. Pin the clay pot bottom in place, pulling the running base stitch to match up the edges. Whip stitch around outside edge to attach the clay pot bottom.

4 Prepare the dirt. Cut a 1.5 liter plastic bottle 4½" (11.5cm) from the bottom, and save the bottom piece. Use fabric glue to attach the dirt base to the cut liter bottle bottom.

5 Add the clay pot. Slip the dirt base liter bottle assembly into the top of the clay pot. Now you can plant your carrot or broccoli by pushing them through the dirt slit.

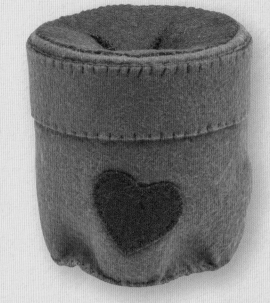

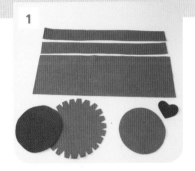

My Secret Garden Patterns

Enlarge Broccoli and Carrot patterns by 190% for actual size

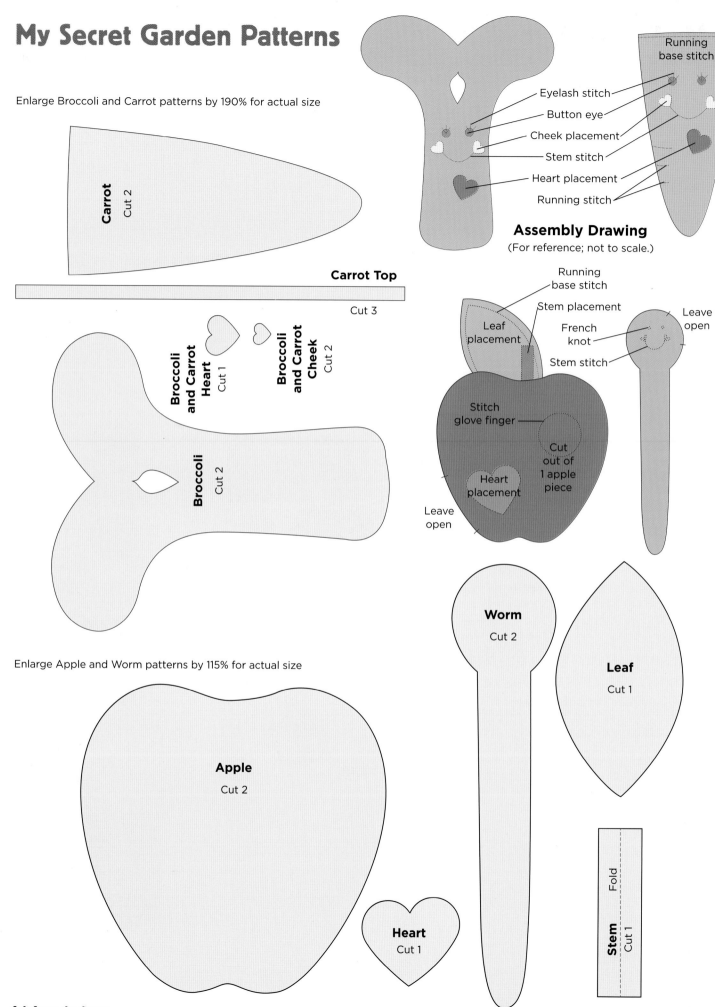

Carrot
Cut 2

Carrot Top
Cut 3

Broccoli and Carrot Heart
Cut 1

Broccoli and Carrot Cheek
Cut 2

Broccoli
Cut 2

Running base stitch

Eyelash stitch
Button eye
Cheek placement
Stem stitch
Heart placement
Running stitch

Assembly Drawing
(For reference; not to scale.)

Running base stitch
Leaf placement
Stem placement
French knot
Leave open
Stem stitch

Stitch glove finger
Cut out of 1 apple piece
Heart placement
Leave open

Enlarge Apple and Worm patterns by 115% for actual size

Apple
Cut 2

Worm
Cut 2

Leaf
Cut 1

Heart
Cut 1

Stem
Cut 1
Fold

My Secret Garden Patterns (continued)

Copy Three Peas in a Pod patterns
at 100% for actual size

Pod
Cut 3
Pea
Cut 6
Cheek #1
Cut 2
Cheek #2
Cut 2
Pea Heart
Cut 3
Pod Heart
Cut 1

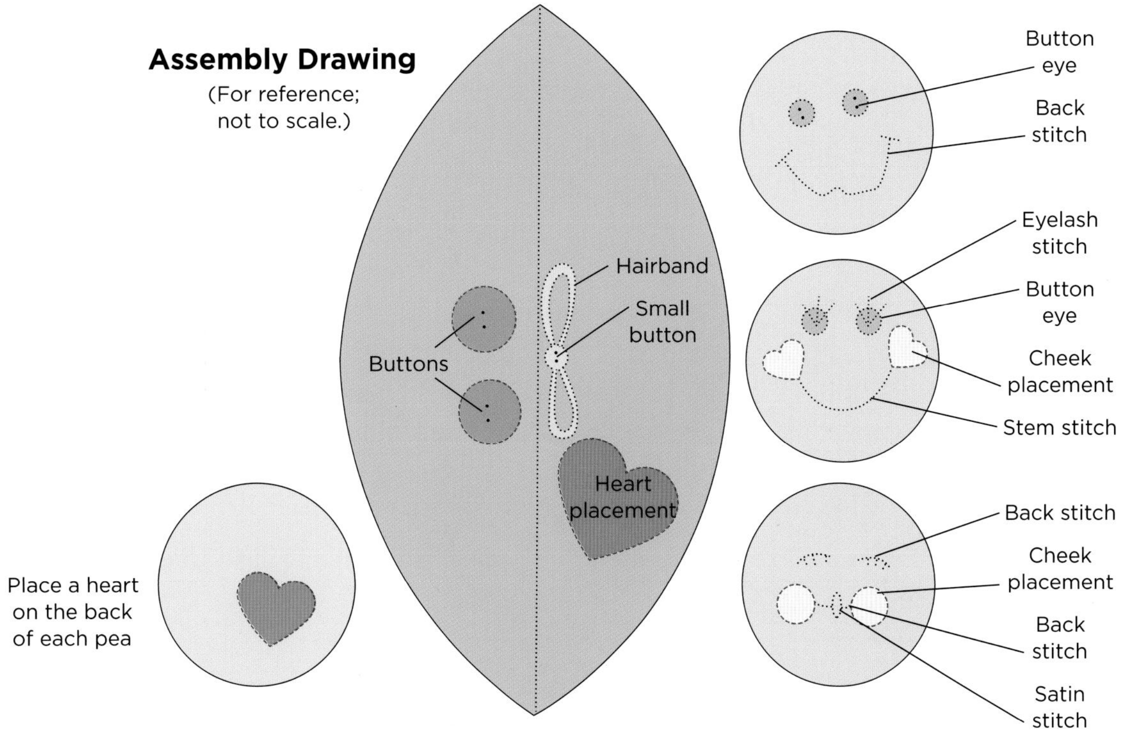

Assembly Drawing
(For reference; not to scale.)
Buttons
Hairband
Small button
Heart placement
Place a heart on the back of each pea
Button eye
Back stitch
Eyelash stitch
Button eye
Cheek placement
Stem stitch
Back stitch
Cheek placement
Back stitch
Satin stitch

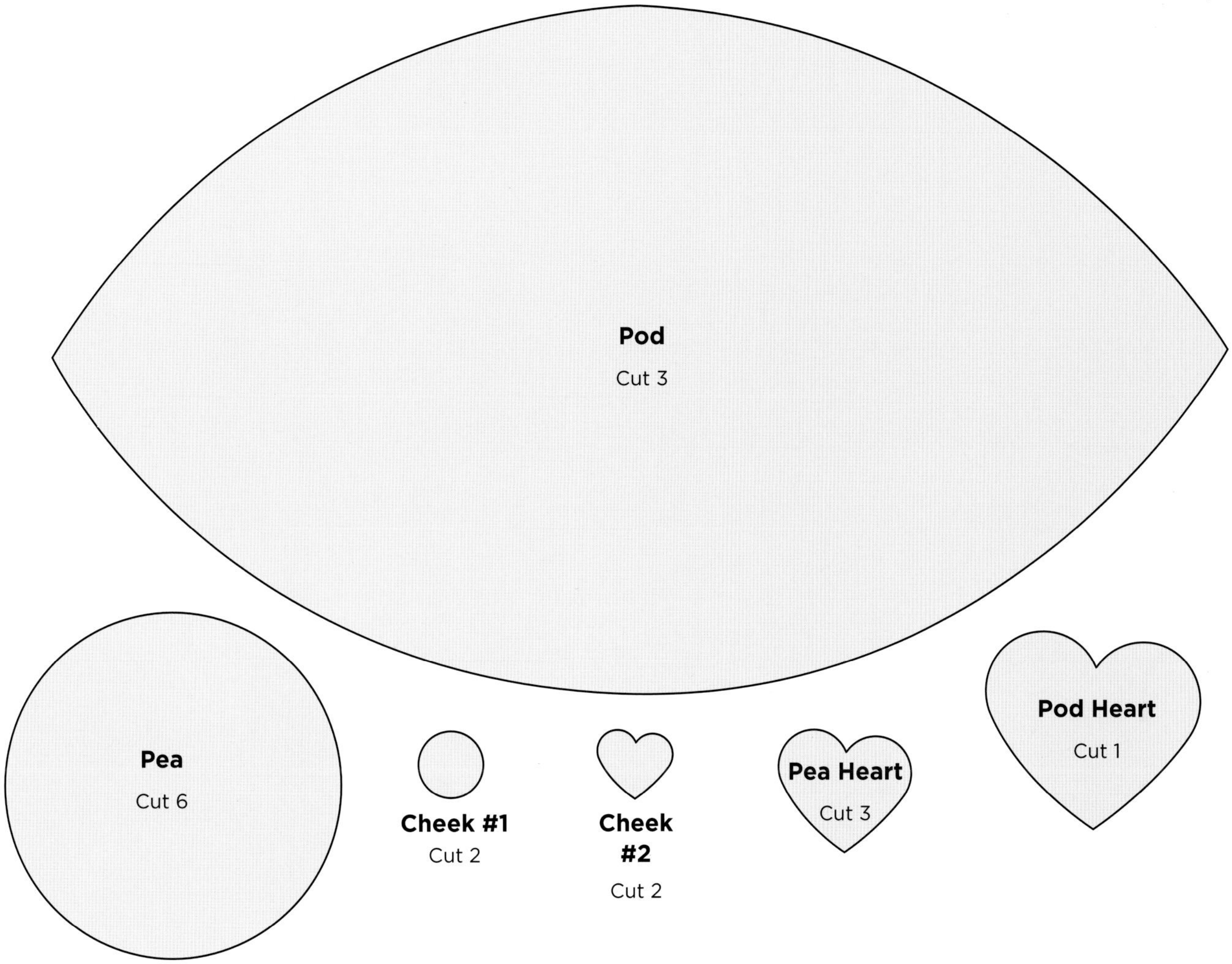

My Secret Garden Patterns (continued)

Enlarge Butterfly patterns by 145% for actual size

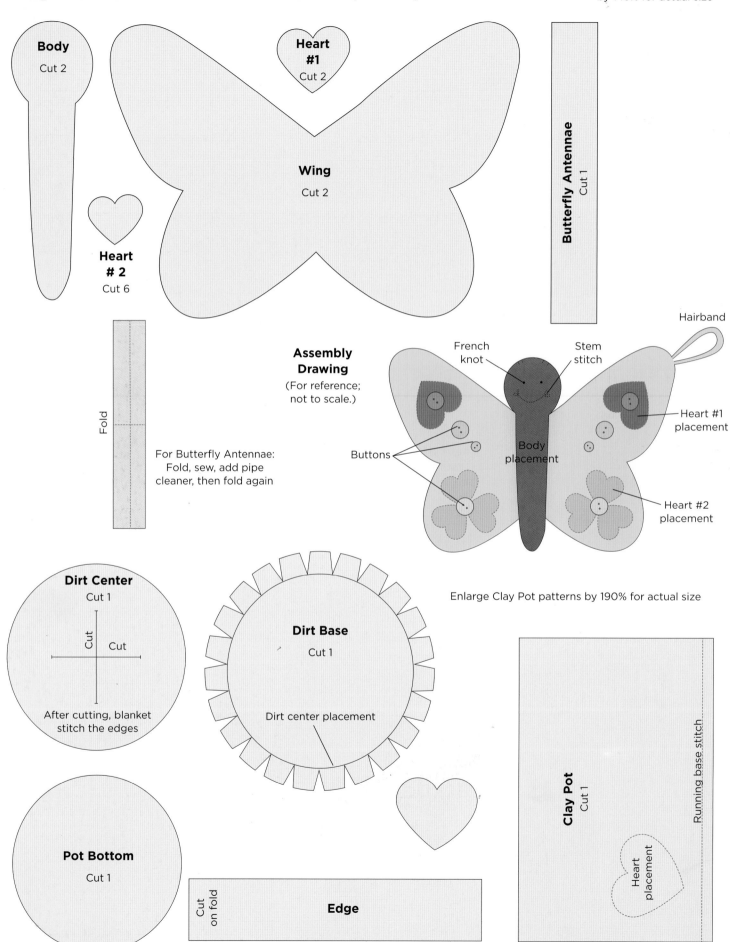

Body
Cut 2

Heart #1
Cut 2

Wing
Cut 2

Butterfly Antennae
Cut 1

Heart # 2
Cut 6

Fold

Assembly Drawing
(For reference; not to scale.)

For Butterfly Antennae:
Fold, sew, add pipe cleaner, then fold again

Hairband

French knot

Stem stitch

Buttons

Body placement

Heart #1 placement

Heart #2 placement

Dirt Center
Cut 1

Cut

Cut

After cutting, blanket stitch the edges

Dirt Base
Cut 1

Dirt center placement

Enlarge Clay Pot patterns by 190% for actual size

Clay Pot
Cut 1

Running base stitch

Heart placement

Pot Bottom
Cut 1

Cut on fold

Edge

Cut on fold